Methamphetamine
Unsafe Speed

ILLICIT AND MISUSED DRUGS

ILLICIT AND MISUSED DRUGS

Methamphetamine
Unsafe Speed

By Kim Etingoff

Mason Crest

Mason Crest
370 Reed Road
Broomall, Pennsylvania 19008
www.masoncrest.com

Printed in the Hashemite Kingdom of Jordan.

First printing
9 8 7 6 5 4 3 2 1

Library of Congress Cataloging-in-Publication Data

Etingoff, Kim.
Methamphetamine : unsafe speed / Kim Etingoff.
    p. cm. — (Illicit and misused drugs)
Includes bibliographical references and index.
ISBN 978-1-4222-2436-6 (hardcover)
ISBN 978-1-4222-2455-7 (paperback)
ISBN 978-1-4222-2424-3 (series hardcover)
ISBN 978-1-4222-9300-3 (ebook)
 1. Methamphetamine abuse—Popular works. I. Title.
HV5822.A5E85 2012
362.29'95—dc23
                                        2011032570

Interior design by Benjamin Stewart.
Cover design by Torque Advertising + Design.
Produced by Harding House Publishing Services, Inc.
www.hardinghousepages.com

CONTENTS

INTRODUCTION

Addicting drugs are among the greatest challenges to health, well-being, and the sense of independence and freedom for which we all strive—and yet these drugs are present in the everyday lives of most people. Almost every home has alcohol or tobacco waiting to be used, and has medicine cabinets stocked with possibly outdated but still potentially deadly drugs. Almost everyone has a friend or loved one with an addiction-related problem. Almost everyone seems to have a solution neatly summarized by word or phrase: medicalization, legalization, criminalization, war-on-drugs.

For better and for worse, drug information seems to be everywhere, but what information sources can you trust? How do you separate misinformation (whether deliberate or born of ignorance and prejudice) from the facts? Are prescription drugs safer than "street" drugs? Is occasional drug use really harmful? Is cigarette smoking more addictive than heroin? Is marijuana safer than alcohol? Are the harms caused by drug use limited to the users? Can some people become addicted following just a few exposures? Is treatment or counseling just for those with serious addiction problems?

These are just a few of the many questions addressed in this series. It is an empowering series because it provides the information and perspectives that can help people come to their own opinions and find answers to the challenges posed by drugs in their own lives. The series also provides further resources for information and assistance, recognizing that no single source has all the answers. It should be of interest and relevance to areas of study spanning biology, chemistry, history, health, social studies and more. Its efforts to provide a real-world context for the information that is clearly presented but not overly simplified should be appreciated by students, teachers, and parents.

The series is especially commendable in that it does not pretend to pose easy answers or imply that all decisions can be made on the basis of simple facts: some challenges have no immediate or simple solutions, and some solutions will need to rely as much upon basic values as basic facts. Despite this, the series should help to at least provide a foundation of knowledge. In the end, it may help as much by pointing out where the solutions are not simple, obvious, or known to work. In fact, at many points, the reader is challenged to think for him- or herself by being asked what his or her opinion is.

A core concept of the series is to recognize that we will never have all the facts, and many of the decisions will never be easy. Hopefully, however, armed with information, perspective, and resources, readers will be better prepared for taking on the challenges posed by addictive drugs in everyday life.

— *Jack E. Henningfield, Ph.D.*

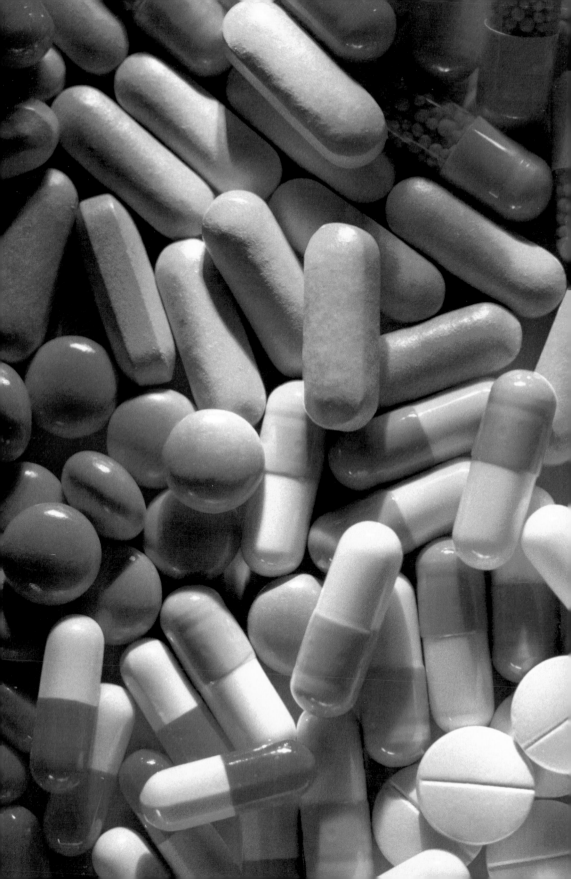

1 What Is Methamphetamine?

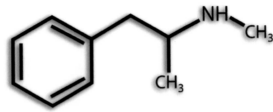

The first time Maggie tried crystal meth, she was terrified. She only took it because her friends were all doing it at a party, and she hated to make a fuss when they kept telling her to give it a try. Once she stopped being scared, though, she liked it. So at the next party, she did it again. And then again. Before long, she wasn't waiting for a party. Meth was making her feel good every day.

When Maggie hit thirteen and started menstruating, she also started gaining weight. From being a skinny little tomboy, she had turned into a chunky young woman. She had hated her new body, and depression had hung over her like a cloud. But now, suddenly, she was losing weight without even trying. And her depression disappeared when she was high. Her friends called it "tweak." It made Maggie feel talkative and energetic. She loved it.

But then her life started falling apart. The weight kept coming off, but it was too much now: when she looked

A nice, well-kept home can hide a multitude of problems, including alcoholism, physical abuse, and drug dependency.

at herself in the mirror, she saw a skeleton with thin, wispy hair. The hanks of hair that fell out when she took a shower scared her. Lots of things were scaring her, especially the thought that she might get caught using meth. She started hiding in her room for days at a time, refusing to come out even to eat. Her parents couldn't understand what was going on, and she ended up screaming at them whenever they tried to talk to her.

Her parents' lives started falling apart as well. Although both her parents had good jobs and they looked like the image of a successful middle-class family, behind the walls of their big house in their pretty suburb, their life was full of turmoil. Maggie's father was drinking too much, Maggie's mother was depressed, and Maggie's little brother was getting into trouble of his own, trying to get his parents' attention.

But Maggie just kept using meth. One night's-worth cost her twenty dollars, and she could easily afford that on her allowance. Half the time, her friends shared with her and she didn't have to pay anything.

When the school called Maggie's parents and told them she hadn't been showing up for classes, her parents hit the roof. They confronted Maggie and insisted she tell them what was going on. At first she lied to them and made excuses, but eventually she confessed the truth. They were horrified; as bad as their lives with Maggie had become, they had never guessed the truth. They grounded her and said she would no longer be allowed to see her friends.

Maggie started sneaking out of her bedroom at night, after her parents thought she was asleep. At first, she tried not to use meth as often, but before long, she was back to using it every day. Sometimes, her friends would give her some for free before school; when her grandmother sent her money for her birthday, she used it to buy all her friends tweak, so that they would return the favor when she needed it.

But eventually, her friendships started to break down as well. She felt jumpy and nervous all the time, and she didn't trust anyone, even her friends. Wherever she went, whatever she was doing, she had a creepy, antsy feeling that people were staring at her, laughing at her, keeping track of everything she was doing. Then she started to see things that weren't there. Her life had turned into a nightmare.

Now that she didn't trust her friends anymore, she couldn't get meth as easily. Desperate, she took her mother's bank card and withdrew money from a cash machine. Her little brother found out what she had done and told her parents; the scene that followed made Maggie decide to leave home.

She ran away from home. Meanwhile, her parents searched everywhere for her. They finally realized that their family was in big trouble. They needed help. Meth was ruining their lives.

Methamphetamine, a man-made substance, belongs to a class of drugs referred to as stimulants. Stimulants are so-called because they speed up the brain's activities, increase energy, and boost alertness. They include such drugs as cocaine and caffeine. Methamphetamine, like other stimulants, creates feelings of pleasure and **euphoria** whether it is taken in pill form, smoked, injected, or inhaled.

Physically, methamphetamine decreases the need for sleep and increases heart rate, breathing rate, and blood pressure. Soon after taking it, the user begins to experience a rush or a high, which accompanies these effects. Most people who use meth want to achieve this desired result. This, coupled with the fact that meth is highly addictive, has led to a high rate of abuse during the last few decades, and makes methamphetamine abuse one of the world's major health concerns of the twenty-first century.

Methamphetamine is also commonly known as meth, speed, chalk, glass, yaba, or ice (when used in its smokable form). Today, methamphetamine is seen as a dangerous drug and a significant threat to society as a result of the increasing prevalence of its abuse. But despite its obvious dangers, it has not always been viewed as a harmful substance.

Methamphetamine can be snorted, popped, smoked, or shot up. The body is "revved up," often with a feeling of intense pleasure.

Methamphetamine—Unsafe Speed

Drug use, including meth, has escalated in North America. In 2006, the DEA sponsored an exhibition warning about the dangers of drug use.

Yaba is one name for methamphetamine, referring to the caffeinated tablet form of the drug that is often colorful and flavored. The name comes from the Thai word for meth. As can be deduced from the origin of its name, this type of meth is made in Southeast Asia and sent by mail to other places around the world, including the United States. Today, it is becoming more popular in Asian communities in western states such as California.

The History of Meth

Meth is a relatively new drug, since it is *synthesized* rather than derived from naturally occurring materials. Amphetamine, the forerunner of methamphetamine, was first created in Germany in 1887. A Japanese pharmacologist later synthesized methamphetamine in 1919. When it became available to the public during the 1930s, it was widely used as a treatment for asthma. However, it was soon used for reasons other than medical treatment, partly in response to the Great Depression of that decade; people turned to methamphetamine to help them cope with their worries and financial stress. People began to notice that the drug also had an effect on wakefulness and alertness, and it was used to this advantage during World War II. Both the Allied and the Axis powers distributed amphetamine tablets to soldiers in an effort to maintain their troops' energy during long periods of fighting. Later, they were used in the Vietnam War and even during the United States' Operation Desert Storm in 1991.

After the conclusion of these wars, many soldiers remained dependent on meth. Particularly in Japan after World War II, meth abuse quickly became an epidemic after war supplies of the drug became available to the public. Combined with the abuse of weight-loss prescription amphetamines, this led to a sharp spike in abuse during the 1950s and '60s. The 1960s also marked the point at which users began the practice of injecting amphet-amines.

The next decade saw a decline in meth abuse as a result of new laws. The Controlled Substance Act of 1970 was put in place in response to the country's growing drug problem and was somewhat successful. Among other things, it regulated the manufacture of amphetamines, making it more difficult for people to access or synthesize them. Meth was also declared a Schedule II drug. Under this classification, meth is recognized as a substance with minimal medical use, but a high potential for abuse.

While the Controlled Substance Act did much to put an end to meth abuse, today this drug is still a worldwide concern. Countries in North America and Asia have especially been affected by widespread use. The problem is not contained within one country; illegal drug trafficking often takes place across borders. For example, much of the meth sold in the United States is originally produced in Mexico and smuggled across the border.

On June 1, 2006, George W. Bush's administration announced a new, global plan to help combat meth. In order to achieve a goal of cutting meth abuse by 15 percent, the administration stated that it would join with the Mexican government to work harder to eliminate illegal smuggling from one country to the other. Since then, the US and Mexico has been cracking down on meth.

How Does Meth Work?

No matter where it is produced or consumed, meth functions the same way in the human body. Meth alters a person's behavior because it works directly on the brain, specifically targeting neurotransmitters. Neurotransmit-

Methamphetamine can help people stay alert for longer periods of time. During World War II, soldiers on both sides of the conflict sometimes used it to stay sharp for battle.

Methamphetamine—Unsafe Speed

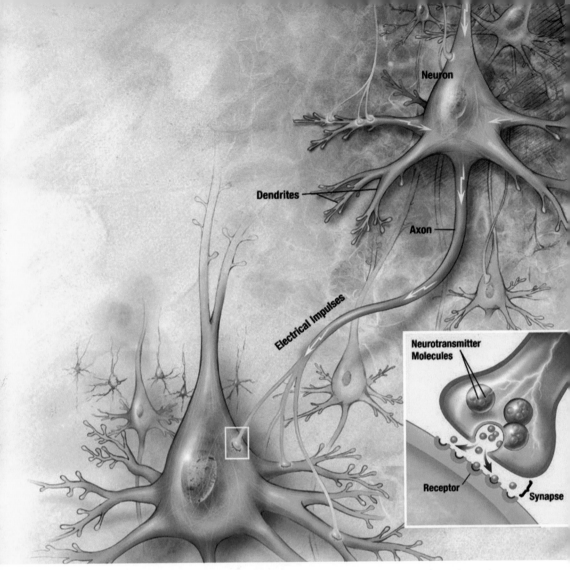

Neuron

Dendrites

Axon

Electrical Impulses

Neurotransmitter Molecules

Receptor

Synapse

Neurons are the mode of transportation for messages moving throughout the brain. Drugs such as methamphetamine can change how those messages are perceived.

ters are chemicals found in the brain that send signals between **neurons**, allowing the brain to relay messages to the rest of the body. Meth interferes with the normal production and transmission of the neurotransmitter called dopamine. Only one of dozens of neurotransmitters, dopamine is involved in the regulation of mood and pleasure. Methamphetamine increases the amount of dopamine found in the brain, causing elated moods and what are essentially feelings of extreme happiness. These artificially elevated feelings initially keep people coming back for more, eventually leading to psychological addiction.

Although meth and cocaine are both stimulants and work in the same way, meth remains in the body for a much longer period of time. Because the chemical takes longer to break down, it affects a user for an extended period of time. It can continue to affect the nervous system anywhere from four hours to as many as twenty-four hours.

The speed at which a user begins to feel the effects of meth depends on the method of use. The faster the drug is introduced into the bloodstream, the quicker the user will feel the results. Injection, which puts meth directly into the bloodstream, produces results after only ten to fifteen seconds. Those who smoke it feel the rush it creates after about the same amount of time. If a person inhales it, they will feel its effects in about three to five minutes. It can also be taken orally in the form of pills or after having been dissolved in a liquid and drunk. More rarely, powdered meth will be sprinkled onto food. This method of use results in a delay of fifteen to twenty minutes before the drug begins to affect the brain, since

Other neurotransmitters and their roles in the body:

- acetylcholine: stimulates muscles, aids in sleep cycle
- norepinephrine: similar to adrenaline, increases heart rate; helps form memories
- GABA (gamma-aminobutyric acid): prevents anxiety
- glutamate: aids in memory formation
- serotonin: regulates mood and emotion
- endorphin: necessary for pleasure and pain reduction

it must be absorbed into the body through the digestive tract. The intensity of the feelings after taking meth also varies with use. Instead of the immediate rush created by injection or smoking, inhaling or ingesting meth produces a general feeling of being high.

The Meth Cycle

Generally, a person on meth goes through several stages of predictable behavior, from extreme highs to severe lows. This cycle is part of the reason why people become so addicted to meth, and why the drug can ruin their lives. Immediately after taking meth, the user feels a rush, the period involving the most intense exhilarated feelings, as well as increases in heartbeat, *metabolism*, and

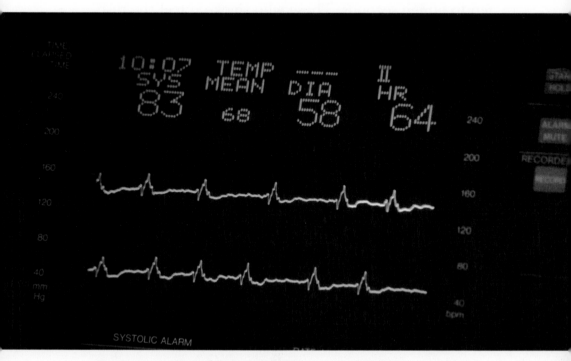

Emotions aren't the only things affected by a meth "high." Heart rates and respiratory rates also increase.

Meth Teachers

Because meth is so easy to make, meth producers are able to teach others how to synthesize the drug. On average, each meth manufacturer teaches ten other people how to make meth each year. This transfer of knowledge increases the amount of meth available to those willing to buy it. It also increases the danger associated with meth labs, since those being taught are not necessarily trained chemists and may not follow safe procedures in the lab, leading to a greater risk of an explosion or contamination of the lab site.

pulse. This stage occurs because meth stimulates a rush of adrenaline, a hormone that causes the body to become hyperalert.

The high, which follows the initial rush, lasts for several hours. In order to maintain this high, users will often binge, meaning that they will continue to take meth for hours, although the rushes they experience aren't as extreme as the first one. The binging stage can last for days at a time, depending on how long the user continues to take the drug.

Eventually users experience what is called "tweaking": after continuous use of meth, it no longer produces any sort of high. During this stage, the user is the most unstable and can become violent or delusional. He or she is unable to sense the effects of the meth they have been taking and feels depressed. Often, alcohol or another drug is used to negate the effects of tweaking, making a tweaker even more dangerous to family, friends, or law enforcement officers.

After tweaking, many users experience a crash. Because they have been using meth for days, they have had little or no sleep and have depleted certain neurotransmitters, such as epinephrine. Their bodies need an incredible amount of sleep to recharge and build up the neurotransmitter to normal, natural levels. Sometimes users crash for as many as three days, sleeping continuously.

Making Meth

The production of methamphetamine is comparatively simple, as well as cheap. The widespread abuse of meth is due in part to the fact that large numbers of people can produce it without a large investment of money or time. Crude and often unsafe labs are set up in homes, cars, and businesses by those eager to make a profit.

Ingredients needed to make meth are not exotic. Most can be found in neighborhood grocery stores and pharmacies.

U.S. Border Patrol agents work with other law enforcement agencies to keep drugs from entering the country.

The chemicals used to make meth are also fairly easy to come by. Pharmacies and grocery stores sell many of the needed ingredients, providing meth manufacturers with easy access to necessary supplies. Drain cleaner, battery acid, antifreeze, and cold medications containing ephedrine can all be used in the production of meth. The ease with which producers can obtain the materials needed for synthesis is a major contributing factor to the growing number of methamphetamine addicts. People no longer have to rely on drug traffickers from other parts of the country or the world. Instead, they can buy meth directly from a local manufacturer.

The groups that actually produce meth have begun to change over the past few years. In the past, motorcycle gangs and other groups based in California and areas in

Ten Reasons Not to Start Using Meth

1. *Meth can mess with your head.*
   Meth can cause users to become delusional, paranoid and suffer from hallucinations. It can also lead to psychotic behavior even months after a user has stopped using. In other words, meth can make you act crazy.

2. *Meth can mess with your social life.*
   Many meth users become so obsessed with using that they neglect their friends and family, which can be a pretty lonely way to live.

3. *Meth can mess with your weight.*
   Meth can decrease one's appetite and cause a person to drop some serious weight, often leaving a user with a sickly, skeleton-like appearance.

4. *Meth can mess with your mouth.*
   Use meth and you can kiss your pearly whites goodbye. While little is known as to why, meth seems to take a terrifying toll on a meth user's mouth. It may be a lack of saliva leaves behind bacteria which can eat away at teeth and gums. Or maybe it's due to the fact that when high on meth, users often neglect personal hygiene and forget to brush their teeth. Either way, meth mouth is pretty gross.

5. *Meth can mess with your neighborhood.*
   Makeshift meth labs can be set up anywhere—from bedrooms to garages to children's play areas to motel rooms—and can cause serious health hazards to you, your family, friends, and neighbors. Cooking meth produces large amounts of highly toxic waste that often gets dumped in yards, alleys, and streets. Meth labs can explode, they can contaminate the environment, and they can endanger children. (Injury from fire, malnutrition, physical and sexual abuse, overdose, and exposure to toxic chemicals are just a few of the possible dangers to children.)

6. *Meth can mess with your moods.*
   Meth can cause extreme mind and mood changes including irritability, anxiety, euphoria, confusion, and severe depression. It can also result in episodes of aggressive and violent behavior.

7. *Meth can mess with your sleep.*
   Because meth stimulates the central nervous system, it can keep users awake and wired all night and even for days after using. When the binge is over, however, most users crash—becoming severely depressed, dis-

oriented, and unable to function. Long-term effects can include chronic fatigue.

8. *Meth can mess with your sex life.*
   Meth can enhance one's sex drive, although, ironically, it can also cause impotence. When high on meth, often the last thing on a user's mind is protection, which can lead to an unplanned pregnancy, or the contraction of HIV/AIDS.

9. *Meth can mess with your skin.*
   Sores and scabs are common among meth users who methodically pick at their skin because they feel compelled to do so, or scratch it because they think there are bugs crawling underneath it.

10. *Meth can kill you.*
    Meth users may experience liver, kidney, lung, and heart problems—all of which can be fatal.

(Source: Partnership for a Drug-Free America)

the southwestern United States manufactured the drug on a large scale. Today, more and more meth is being produced by independent groups or even individuals, in amateur "mom-and-pop" labs. Small quantities of the drug are produced by these labs, rather than the massive quantities made by the older, larger meth manufacturers. More meth is also being produced in Mexico and is making its way illegally across the border into the United States. The growing problem of mom-and-pop meth labs is not limited to the United States. In Canada, thirty meth labs were seized by police in British Columbia, the province with the most significant meth crisis. With the increased prevalence of meth use, the crime rate in British Columbia has also gone up, suggesting a concrete link between meth and criminal activity.

Methamphetamine in Canada

According to the website of the Royal Canadian Mounted Police (www.rc-mp-grc.gc.ca), the use of methamphetamine is growing in Canada. Experts there indicate that the overall use and distribution of meth in the provinces has increased, with some areas noting a "skyrocketing" increase in the drug's prevalence. There has been an especially significant rise in British Columbia and Alberta, although the entire country is facing the effects of meth as it spreads from cities to more rural areas.

Most of the meth being distributed in Canada is produced domestically. The RCMP also reports that Canada has become a player in the trafficking of meth to other countries, including the United States and Japan. Organized crime, motorcycle gangs, and Asian crime groups are involved in the production and distribution of meth.

Canadian law enforcement agencies have cracked down on meth labs throughout the country. In 2008, forty-three meth labs were seized, up from twenty-five in 2002.

While most of the focus on illegal drug trafficking is on the Mexican-American border, smuggling also occurs frequently between the United States and Canada. The United States generally has tighter controls on the sale of chemicals needed to make methamphetamine. Taking advantage of the close proximity of Canada and its looser restrictions, many northern manufacturers buy these chemicals there and smuggle them into the United States.

Some Common Ingredients in Methamphetamine:

starting fluid (ether)
paint thinner
freon
acetone
anhydrous ammonia
iodine crystals
red phosphorous
brake cleaner
drain cleaner (sodium hydroxide)
battery acid (sulfuric acid)
cold medicines containing pseudoephedrine

Using meth is not all about highs. It can cause severe mood swings, even depression.

2 Who Uses Methamphetamine?

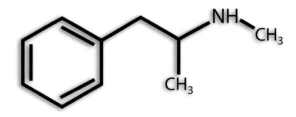

Derek has come a long way since his Harvard days. In the ten years since he graduated with a doctoral degree in business, life hasn't exactly worked out as he had planned. At thirty-seven years old, he's a meth addict. He's been hospitalized several times for meth-induced psychosis, and even when his head is working better, he still suffers from constant depression. His skin is covered with abscesses from injecting the drug.

Derek is a homosexual who mixes meth and risky sex in a dangerous combination that is raising HIV-infection rates. He lives in a dark and shadowy underworld where he has no true friends or lovers, where no one cares about anything but meth.

His life wasn't always this way, of course. He started out with a good job where he made lots of money. But his parents refused to accept his lifestyle, and then his partner broke up with him. Derek sank into a depression.

When he started shooting speed, he felt as though he had found the answer to his emotional issues. Nothing seemed to matter when he was high. Soon, he was using meth every day as a way to escape the burden of his emotions. He didn't realize his life was on a disaster course.

When his boss found out he was using speed at work, Derek lost his job. With no family or friends to care what became of him, he continued his dark spiral downward. By the time he was thirty, he was living in dingy apartment with broken windows, sleeping in his clothes to save on his heating bill. He went on welfare, which meant he had an income of $395 a month; he spent $80 to a $100 of that on speed. His days blurred into one another. Between highs, his moods plunged, and he obsessed over where he would get the money for his next fix.

Derek hated his life. When he wasn't high, he felt lonely, depressed, and guilty. But he didn't know how to change.

While Derek's story is fictional, it is based on several real-life accounts from addicts. The following story, however, by a woman named Jennifer Romano, is completely true. Jennifer shared her story on the Partnership for a Drug-Free America website.

> Meth destroyed me—it cost me my marriage, my relationship with my children, and my friends, and family's trust. Worst of all, it almost cost me the life of my youngest daughter.
>
> I enjoyed a happy childhood growing up in Aurora, Colorado, with two loving parents. I moved to Texas when I was nine, and then back to Colorado when I was fourteen. My parents did

not abuse drugs, I did not live around drug dealers—I didn't even know what a joint was. This innocence, however, soon ended.

I got together with my current ex-husband in 1998, but I had known him since childhood. He was my first love, and I would have done anything for him. He was using drugs and I felt pressure to participate. When we first got married, I smoked cigarettes and weed and drank alcohol. But soon, we began using hard drugs together. We tried cocaine and speed—first snorting, and later smoking it off of tin foil, a lightbulb, and even a glass pipe.

Drugs, including meth, can destroy lives. People who abuse them can lose all they have, including their homes and their dignity.

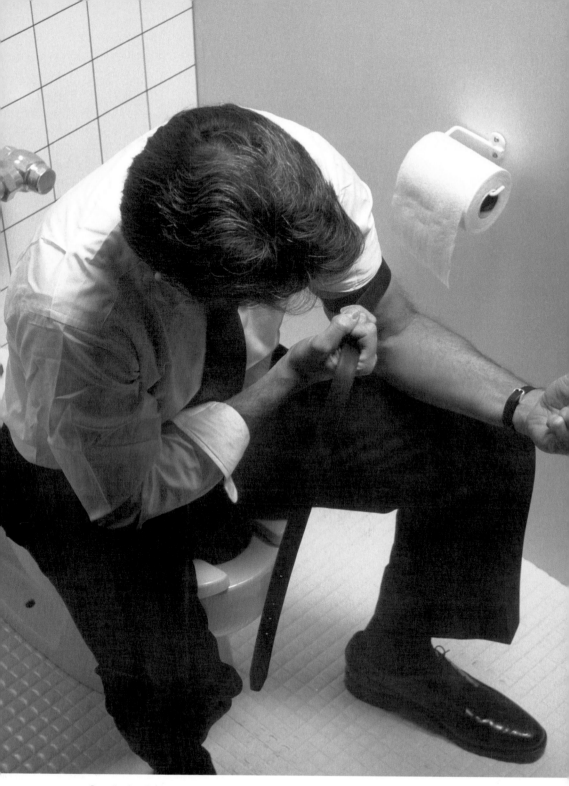

People hooked on meth take advantage of any opportunity to have a fix. It doesn't matter when—or where.

I used meth for the first time in February of 1999. I remember it like it was yesterday—the rush, the warmth coursing through my body from head to toe, a particular taste in the back of my mouth. I thought it was cool that this drug could remain in my system for few days, rather than just a few hours. It didn't take very long for me to start shooting it up on a regular basis.

In April of 1999, my nineteenth birthday, I found out that I was pregnant. I stopped using hard drugs right then and there. My healthy baby girl was born in December, and the first thing I wanted to do after I delivered her was a "bump." Once I did it, I was hooked again. We moved into a new place and tried to make a life for ourselves, but that dream ended when we met our first famous "dope cook" and my husband became a runner for him. Basically, we took him everywhere he needed to go and in return got free drugs. We thought this was the best deal going.

We lost our place in May of 2000 because we used all the drugs we had instead of selling them to pay the rent. On top of this, I found out that I was pregnant again with our second child. We kept running dope for the cook so that we could make some money, but we were caught and my husband went to jail in September for three months and things went downhill from there.

I went into labor with my baby six weeks early, and I think it's because that night, I shot up meth. They kept her in the hospital for two weeks because she could not keep up her body weight. Looking back on it now, I could have seriously harmed my daughter—I don't know what I was thinking! I am so lucky that she is healthy now. Because of all my problems, the hospital released my daughter to my mom. I was able to get her back in January of that year, but that didn't stop me from continuing to abuse meth.

We were moving in and out of houses, staying with our parents and relatives, and using drugs the entire time. We left our children behind because we were so hooked; we thought of nothing else but ourselves and our next fix. We ran into some friends from high school, and began using drugs with them—I even went so far as to tell my friend Lauren to try meth. She was instantly hooked.

My relationship with my husband soon grew sour; we were fighting over money, and I wanted to get out of the drug business. I left him two days before his birthday. He was so upset that he told everyone we knew never to sell me drugs again. I thought I was quitting, but I ran into Lauren shortly after I stopped using and she got me to shoot up again. I knew it wasn't a good idea to go over there, but I couldn't help myself. I only shot up once—but that's all it takes.

I was using off and on for a while. I tried to stay clean, but the urges were just too strong. I had a new boyfriend and I had finally made it a year without using. I thought things were finally going well, but then my ex-husband, who became a dope cook, got out of prison. After seeing him again, I went back to using. Since I was involved with the drug again, my current boyfriend started using. I am now terrified of losing another person I love to this powerful substance. He could not admit that

A drug addiction can cause tension in relationships. Eventually family relationships and friendships can be destroyed.

Methamphetamine—Unsafe Speed 35

Each year many individuals are sentenced to prison for drug-related crimes.
Once released, many reoffend and return to prison for even longer sentences.

he had a problem and I knew that I would never stop if I was with someone who used—so I left.

Now I live in Mabank, Texas, which is battling a meth problem and has been nicknamed "Speeder Creek Lake." There are so many people here who use the drug—I even know people who have been murdered over it. I finally understood what this drug was doing to me, and I knew that I had to stop for good. So I did.

I now battle awful cravings and powerful urges, but I have been clean since November 13, 2004— and every day is just as hard as the previous one. I was able to get clean through my own perseverance and the help of a good friend who I am currently engaged to marry. I've also been attending Alcoholics Anonymous for a couple of months, which has helped me get some solid ground to stand on for my children. My girls live with me, but they have security problems and rely on their grandparents to buy them toys to make them feel better. Now, I am trying to regain their trust by spending time with them and playing games and watching movies—I desperately want to rebuild our relationship.

Meth makes people's lives a living hell. I have done the "picking" which left sores all over my body. When I popped them, they left scars. I have had suicidal thoughts; I have been paranoid and made a complete fool of myself by becoming so obsessed with a drug that I neglected my children. No one made me shoot up meth but me—I called it my "demon of choice." I know I am addicted, now all I have to do is be more powerful than the drug—not only for myself, but for my kids.

I am not just someone you read about—I am a real person, an addicted person. I can only hope that my story is found by those who need it, and that they can learn from my mistakes and save their own lives.

All sorts of people use meth: kids and adults, men and women. For example, in an e-mail sent to KCI: The Anti-Meth Site, Holly Q. discussed how meth abuse ripped her family apart. She thought her life was perfectly in order: she had recently been married, enjoyed a loving relationship with her husband, and had two healthy sons. However, despite celebrating the birth of their second son and starting a promising construction partnership, something was wrong with her husband, Craig. He seemed depressed and tense, unlike his usual manner. He eventually admitted to Holly that he was addicted to meth, but he agreed to quit. A few years later, after their third son was born, Craig again fell into the same depression as before. He checked himself into a drug treatment facility, although he had to return home since there was a waiting period before he could enter. During that waiting period, things got worse.

Unable to deal with living with Craig anymore, Holly took her children to live with her parents, later selling the house she and Craig had lived in. The two eventually divorced, although he occasionally sees his children.

Clearly, the abusers of methamphetamine do not all fit the common stereotype attached to drug users: they are not necessarily poor, urban youth. Craig, a fairly well-off, young father with a stable family life, used meth with devastating effects. Users often belong to surprising categories of people.

Someone who shows signs of being depressed may actually be addicted to drugs. Depression is just one symptom of addiction, however.

No Common User

Addiction to meth cannot be predicted by typical means such as gender or location. Males and females use it on an approximately equal basis, and it is no more common in cities than in rural areas. In other words, a wide variety of people abuse meth.

However, there are some general groups that tend to use methamphetamine more often. Although it is now changing, the traditional profile of an abuser is a white, middle-aged, *blue-collar* worker. Instead of using meth solely for the sake of the sensation it produces, these

In 2010, the National Survey on Drug Use and Health reported that 105,000 Americans twelve and older had tried meth for the first time in the past year. This number is higher than the number of first-time users in 2008 (95,000), but lower than the number of first-time users in 2002 (299,000).

Many young people first try meth at raves. But, it's important to remember that there isn't just one profile of a meth abuser.

working individuals often take meth to work longer, more productive hours. Because meth causes a decrease in the need for sleep, they see it as an easy way to stay awake, work more efficiently, and make more money.

More and more younger people have begun to use meth as well. It has become a popular drug at **rave parties**, which have introduced it to millions of new users. Students, both at high schools and colleges, also use the drug, but often for reasons other than recreation: similar to their adult counterparts, they use it as a study aid to help them stay awake, allowing them to maintain energy when they become too drained to study on their own. In fact, studies have shown that teenagers generally believe that meth is safer than other drugs, such as cocaine, and as a result, they don't think of it as a "serious" drug.

Some users begin taking meth as a weight-loss aid. Meth functions as an appetite suppressant and causes a relatively quick drop in weight. While this weight loss can become extreme, many people, especially younger women, see this as a benefit and take the drug specifically for this effect. These same people may then become addicted to their weight-loss plan.

Of course, not every person looking to work more efficiently or lose weight uses meth. And not every person who does use meth falls under any of these categories.

Geographic Division

In the past, most users of meth lived on the West Coast. Originally, recreational use of the drug first took its toll in Hawaii, the habit being imported from Southeast Asia. From there, it spread to California and eventually to the entire western coast of the United States.

Methamphetamine is becoming increasingly popular in the gay club scene in larger cities like New York. The most common form of taking the drug is through injections, increasing the risk of the spread of HIV among clubbers.

However, this geographical trend is quickly changing. Meth use is spreading throughout the country and is slowly moving its way east, although for now, abuse, as well as production, is still significantly higher in the west. According to the Community **Epidemiology** Work Group, the four cities with the highest percentages of adult males arrested who tested positive for meth were all located in the West Coast or Southwest regions of the United States.

Once more prevalent in cities, meth use is now more balanced between urban and rural areas. In order to avoid arrest in the urban centers where police may be actively looking for those involved with drugs, traffickers often target more rural areas. The Midwest has especially felt the impact of their activity, and the number of meth users is particularly growing in this region, as well as in the South. Some figures report that as many as 90 percent of all drug cases in the Midwest are related to meth.

Geography not only affects the actual use of meth; it also impacts the method of use that is most popular. For instance, in San Francisco, the majority of users inject the drug; in Hawaii, users typically smoke it. In Phoenix, Arizona, older meth users snort the drug, and younger ones ingest it in pill form.

Categories of Users

Meth abusers generally fall into one of three categories: low intensity, binge, or high intensity. Low intensity is often used to describe those who casually take the drug for a reason other than recreation. This type of user includes people using meth as a study or weight-loss aid, or to work extra shifts at a job. Low-intensity abusers generally take meth orally or by snorting, since they are not looking to use it for its euphoric effects. Nonetheless, low-intensity abuse is still a concern, since using meth at a low intensity can easily act as a stepping-stone to more serious abuse.

Binge and high-intensity users take meth much more often than low-intensity users. They also look to experience the euphoria it produces, so they inject or smoke it to produce a longer and more intense rush. High-intensity abuse is the most serious category. A high-intensity

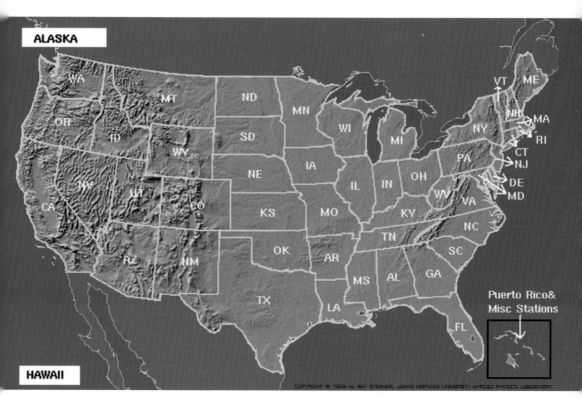

Crystal meth use began in Hawaii and stayed on the West Coast for many years. Now, its use is spreading across the United States.

Not all methamphetamine is illegal. When prescribed by a health-care professional, it can be used to treat many conditions, including narcolepsy and obesity.

abuser usually cannot lead a normal life because of his or her addiction and need for continual meth use. These people are often violent, especially if they are coming off the high, and they are the most prone to the many health risks involved with meth.

Legal Users

Not everyone who uses meth can be labeled an abuser; methamphetamine also has accepted medical value. While it must be prescribed with great care, it is currently used under the name Desoxyn as a treatment for attention-deficit disorder, *narcolepsy*, and some types of depression. With the advent of newer medications, and the growth of awareness of the drug's abuse, however, the use of medicinal meth is declining in favor of other drugs that can treat the same problems.

Ironically, meth is also sometimes used as a treatment for obesity because of its ability to act as an appetite suppressant. While some people abuse meth in order to lose what they feel are extra pounds, those who are prescribed meth by a doctor are legitimately obese, that is, a man whose weight is 20 percent or a woman whose weight is 25 percent over the maximum desirable weight for height. In their cases, the risks of disease and death from obesity outweigh the risks of the methamphetamine they are given.

How Can Users Be Identified?

There are certain characteristics and behaviors that can be used to determine if someone is a *chronic* abuser of meth. Physically, he or she may speak very quickly and incoherently, have *dilated* pupils and bloodshot eyes,

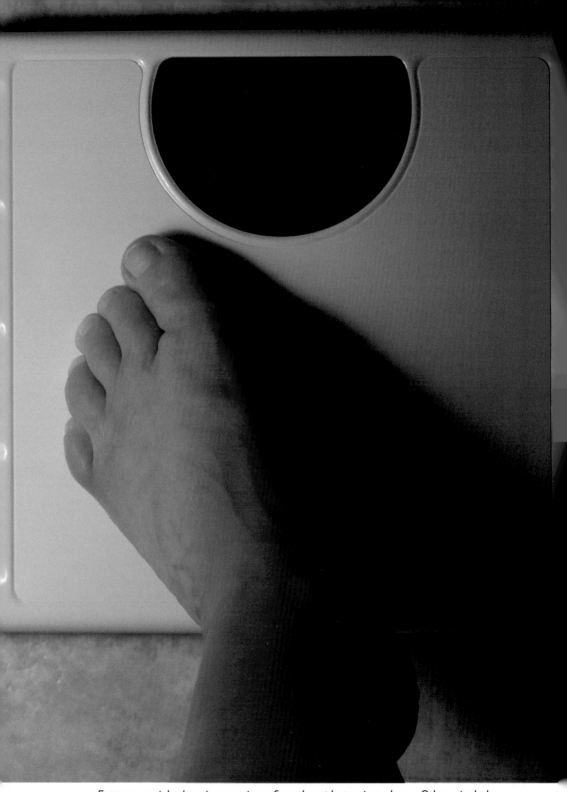

Extreme weight loss is one sign of methamphetamine abuse. Others include bloodshot eyes and meth mouth.

sweat a lot, lose weight over a short period of time, have stained teeth (meth mouth), or have unexplained scars. Before and after pictures of meth addicts are often shocking because the drug has changed their appearance so radically.

Abusers' actions also point to their addiction. Some users have paranoia and hallucinations, lose their memories, become depressed, grind their teeth, and/or seem to always be restless and tense.

How Much Do You Know About Meth?

(answers on page 50–51)

1. Meth is made from:
a) only natural products from the earth.
b) paint thinner, battery acid and cat litter.
c) caffeine and sugar.
d) cocaine.

2. The meth problem exists:
a) only in the Midwest.
b) only in rural communities.
c) in numerous cities and towns across America.
d) only on spring break.

3. Meth has the ability to:
a) make problems disappear permanently.
b) cause delusions and violent rages.
c) relieve common cold symptoms.
d) help you ace algebra without ever studying for a test.

4. Meth labs are:
a) found in chemistry classrooms in select high schools.
b) where meth users conduct science experiments.
c) completely safe and totally harmless to children and the environment.
d) often located in a basement, garage or even a bedroom or car.

5. If a person uses meth for a long time, he or she:
a) can damage his or her internal organs, which can lead to kidney and heart failure.
b) will become the valedictorian.
c) have a smaller chance of becoming addicted.
d) will get it for free since he or she is such a loyal user.

6. Meth cooks are:
a) gourmet chefs in four-star restaurants.
b) people who use meth as an ingredient in their everyday recipes.
c) people who illegally produce meth in their own home.
d) a new indie-rock band.

7. If you only use meth a few times, you:
a) will make a lot more friends.
b) might think bugs are crawling under your skin, and scratch at your body to get rid of them.
c) will build up a tolerance toward other drugs.
d) won't get in as much trouble with the law if you are caught.

8. Common slang terms for meth are:
a) tina and chalk.
b) blow and nose candy.
c) dope and smack.
d) grass and hash.

9. Meth is:
a) a stimulant.
b) an illegal drug.
c) addictive.
d) all of the above.

(Source: Partnership for a Drug-Free America)

Answers:

1. (B): Meth is made from some pretty nasty products. Among paint thinner, battery acid and cat litter, there is also iodine, kerosene, and drain cleaner, just to name a few more. (A) is incorrect because there aren't too many natural products which go into this drug (not that it would make it all right, since, for example, heroin is made from a natural product—the poppy plant—but it still has devastating effects on the body and mind and can even kill you). (C) and (D) are trick answers because the effects meth has on the body can resemble a caffeine or sugar high—and even a cocaine high. However, while meth is an upper like these other substances, it can cause users to stay high for hours and even days, harming their body and causing them to become disoriented and unstable in the process, something caffeine and sugar do not do. A cocaine high, although just as dangerous, is different because it lasts for a shorter time.

2. (C): Meth production, sales, and addiction are problems that are now affecting communities across America. Although meth was once found in predominantly rural, Midwestern towns and West Coast cities, it should no longer be associated with these areas. Although meth could be used on a spring break trip, there are unfortunately many more places than a tropical island where abuse takes place.

3. (B): Chronic meth use can cause hallucinations, delusions, and violent behavior as it affects the central nervous system. (C) is incorrect—even though meth is made from pseudoephedrine, an ingredient in over-the-counter cold medication, it will in no way relieve the symptoms from the common cold. (A) is incorrect because meth itself will not make a person's problems go away. Meth addicts will often abuse the drug as a way to self-medicate, but it's never a permanent solution to any problem; it just generates more issues, such as health problems and addiction. Most likely a meth user would be too busy thinking about where to get his next fix and forget to study for his calculus test, and would probably not ace the course.

4. (D): Meth labs can often go undetected in regular, suburban neighborhoods, as meth cooks can produce large amounts of the drug in the comfort of their own home. This is highly dangerous and illegal. (A) is incorrect as most schools regulate what type of experiments go on in their classrooms, and while (B) sounds interesting, most meth cooks have their "recipe" down to a science and aren't experimenting. (C) is also wrong, since the opposite is true: meth labs are extremely dangerous to members of a community, its children, and the surrounding environment due to the hazardous materials that are used in the making of meth.

5. (A): Meth puts a huge strain on a user's internal organs as it drastically affects the central nervous system. Since the body is working overtime, there is an increased risk of heart failure and death associated with this drug. (B) is incorrect because the longer a person uses meth, the less concerned she will be about her schoolwork, and the more occupied she will become with finding her next fix, which is also why (C) is wrong: the more you use this drug, the more likely you will become addicted. Also, don't let (D) fool you—meth might be cheaper than some other drugs, but it's hardly ever free, it's highly addictive, and it can lead to serious physical and mental harm. And in no time, every dollar you can get your hands on will be going to feed your habit, not your body.

6. (C): An eerie fact of the meth business is that it takes place in the neighborhoods in which you're supposed to feel safe. Meth cooks are just ordinary citizens who illegally make an addictive and sometimes lethal substance right inside their own homes. They don't need to be a gourmet chef (A) to understand the recipe, and meth is not used as an ingredient in everyday recipes (B).

7. (B): Common side effects meth users may experience are hallucinations, which can include the feeling that bugs are crawling underneath their skin. Since they're usually too preoccupied with scratching away these imagined bugs, meth users don't have much time to be making new friends, which is why (A) is incorrect. (C) is tricky but wrong. Although many drug users tend to build up a "tolerance" to their drug of choice, it does not mean that they aren't damaging their bodies by continuing to use that drug or others. The tolerance users experience makes them feel the need to do a drug much more frequently to get the effect they desire. While using drugs more frequently increases one's chances of being caught, it doesn't mean that you won't get in trouble the first time you try it. Also, regardless of the number of times you've used meth, if you're caught with it, you can be charged with possession, the same as a heavy user could be, which is why (D) is incorrect.

8. (A): Meth is commonly referred to as tina and chalk, as well as crystal, ice, glass, and crank. (B) lists slang terms for cocaine, while (C) and (D) refer to street names for heroin and marijuana respectively.

9. (D): As you probably have learned already, meth is a stimulant, it's highly addictive, and it's illegal. You might want to think twice about trying it. It's a horrible trap you don't want to go anywhere near.

(Source: Partnership for a Drug-Free America)

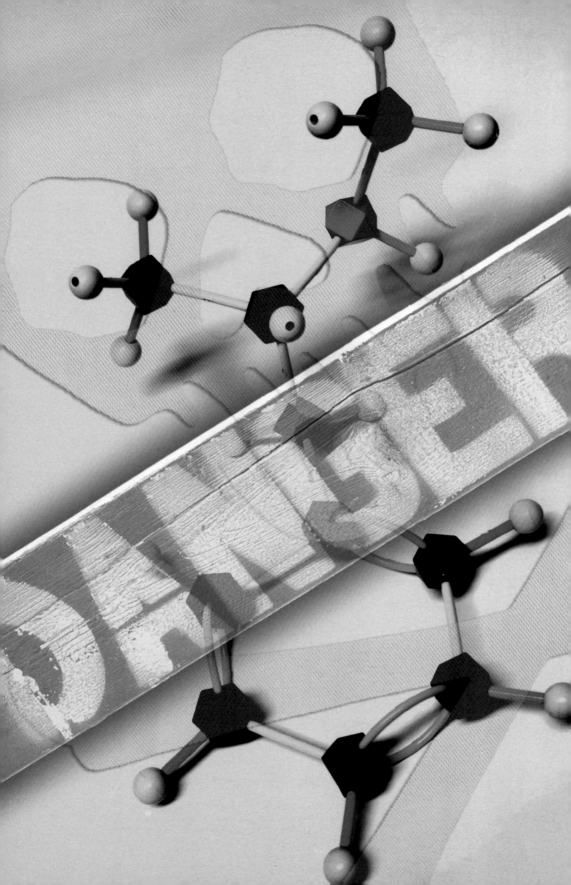

3 What Are the Dangers of Methamphetamine?

If you live in Montana, you may have seen some disturbing ads on television. In one of them, a teenager plucks her eyebrow—and when the camera moves back, you see that she's completely removed her other eyebrow, leaving only a red welt across her forehead. The voice-over says, "It's amazing what you can accomplish on meth."

These harsh and graphic ads are targeted at teenagers by the Montana Meth Project. The project (which is partially funded by software billionaire Thomas Siebel) has plastered anti-meth messages across the state, on billboards and newspapers, and on television and radio.

The Meth Project is trying hard to keep Montana teens from ever trying meth, even once. The radio ads also feature real-life recovering meth addicts telling their stories, while the Meth Project's website includes the personal stories of other users. Caitlin is one of the young people who tells her story in a radio ad.

She tells how she started using meth when she was fifteen, and that one of the worst moments in her entire life happened right after she had used the drug. "I felt like if I even moved one inch, I would have a heart attack, my heart was beating so fast."

Caitlin is clean now, as are the other volunteers who tell their story for the Meth Project. The project is determined to spread the word: meth is dangerous.

A drug can be defined as any substance, other than food, that alters the structure or function of the body. Methamphetamine does exactly that, sometimes severely impairing a person both mentally and physically. Many meth users don't consider what may happen to them in the future as a result of their addiction, or don't take the drug's unpleasant and often life-threatening side effects seriously. However, whether or not they take the side effects into account, chronic abusers will be negatively affected by their habit; it is simply a question of time and intensity of use.

Short-Term Effects

Besides producing a high, meth affects users in other obvious ways. While under the influence of meth, or after habitually using it, a person can develop headaches,

In one laboratory study done on meth addiction, animals pressed levers that released methamphetamine into their bodies. In the end, the animals exclusively pressed these levers, ignoring the food, exercise, and mates that were offered to them. Some even died of starvation, demonstrating the extreme consequences that meth addiction can have on any animal, including humans.

Blurred vision may occur when someone is on meth. This side effect may be completely unexpected by someone taking the drug.

blurred vision, hot flashes, dizziness, dry mouth, tremors, insomnia, and **athetosis**. These side effects, while reducing quality of life, are not even among the most serious of meth's consequences.

When taken in large doses over a short period of time, meth can have even more drastic effects. In some cases, body temperature spikes to dangerously high levels, resulting in a condition known as hyperthermia. This, along with convulsions that can also develop after taking large doses, can result in death.

Meth does not only affect a user physically. Since it acts on the central nervous system, profound behavioral changes can be observed in a person who is high on or addicted to meth. During the rush or high, a person may

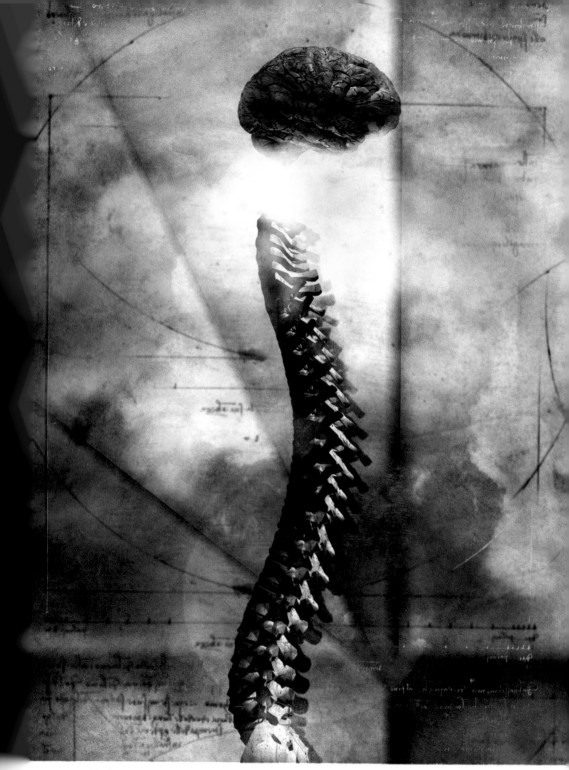

Meth works on the body's central nervous system. Meth abuse can cause tremendous highs followed by confusion and aggression when the drug's effects leave the body.

feel more self-confident and will have high levels of energy and alertness, resulting in changes in behavior and personality. However, after the initial high wears off, meth produces nervousness, irritability, confusion, and aggression. A person may also feel depressed when not on meth, or after coming down from a high, causing him or her to take the drug again, leading to psychological addiction. This feeling of depression is one factor that makes meth addiction hard to break. Besides changes in mood, a common behavioral change frequently reported in meth users is picking at the skin of the face or hands, which can cause scarring over time. This is a reaction to the sensation that bugs are crawling on the skin, a condition known as formication. Other repetitive behaviors, paranoia, and hallucinations may also occur.

Long-Term Effects

The most severe effects of meth become apparent after it has been used over an extended period. Brain damage, some of it irreparable, is one major concern, and can result in memory loss, trouble with movement, and learning impediments, along with death if the damage is critical enough. Research suggests that the cells in the brain that produce the neurotransmitters dopamine and serotonin can be severely damaged, even after relatively light use of methamphetamine. Recovery and regrowth can be extremely slow, and damage may not ever be healed.

Other parts of the body besides the brain are also negatively impacted by meth. **Vascular** problems, including increased heart rate and heart failure, as well as stroke, sometimes become apparent in long-term meth users. These problems are triggered mainly by the dramatic

Symptoms of long-term meth use can mimic those of schizophrenia. Individuals may withdraw from those to whom they were once close.

increase in blood pressure that meth produces, which can strain and cause damage to blood vessels. Kidney, lung, and liver damage can occur, as can problems with the immune system, all of which can lead to death.

Less dangerous, but still of concern, are several other long-term effects. These include dilation of the pupils, tooth grinding, speech problems, dry skin, acne, and excessive sweating. A meth user's appearance is sometimes drastically changed from before the abuse began. Meth causes damage to blood vessels, preventing blood flow to all parts of the body, including the face and skin. Users' teeth also decay, due both to poor hygiene and to the drug itself. However, some scientists suggest that it is not the drug that causes meth mouth. Because abusers become dehydrated, they must quench their thirst and often do so with soda, which causes tooth decay. This exacerbates the dental problem, which isn't helped by the fact that many meth users are not likely to take good care of their teeth.

As with short-term effects, some of the most serious long-term effects are psychological and behavioral. Long-time users of meth can develop the symptoms of *schizophrenia* or drug-induced *psychosis*, withdrawing from their former lives, society, and reality. Sometimes, these problems can be so bad as to cause thoughts of murder and suicide, posing a danger to others as well as to the user himself.

Overdosing

Meth users can overdose (take a lethal amount of a drug). Although the level of meth that constitutes an overdose is different from person to person, low levels of the drug can sometimes be considered toxic. Users with a low tolerance for meth can overdose with as little as fifty milligrams, while that amount may not be as toxic for people who have used meth for longer periods of time and have built up a tolerance. Signs of an overdose include fever, convulsions and tremors, heart problems, and eventually, death.

Immediate hospitalization is required for people who have overdosed. Typically, patients who enter emergency rooms because of meth overdoses are first cooled off to reduce body temperature, which may be at extreme levels, and given drugs to treat convulsions. Anti-anxiety medications are also sometimes used. Then they are usually placed in a quiet, supervised area and allowed to return to a stable condition.

Indirect Danger

Not all of meth's dangers are as obvious as the effects the drug itself has on a person's body and mind. For example, those who inject meth are at risk for HIV/AIDS. Since the disease is transmitted through body fluids, sharing needles that come into contact with an infected person's bloodstream can spread HIV to healthy users. HIV, along with other sexually transmitted diseases, is also spread by meth users because of the effects that the drug has on the mind. A person high on meth is more likely to participate in risky behaviors, such as having unprotected sex, than if she were sober.

Lead poisoning is another risk associated with the use of methamphetamine. Because meth is synthesized in less-than-sterile conditions, and because the producer may be inexperienced, the finished product can contain poisonous impurities such as lead. The impurities are not monitored and are unsuspectingly transferred to users'

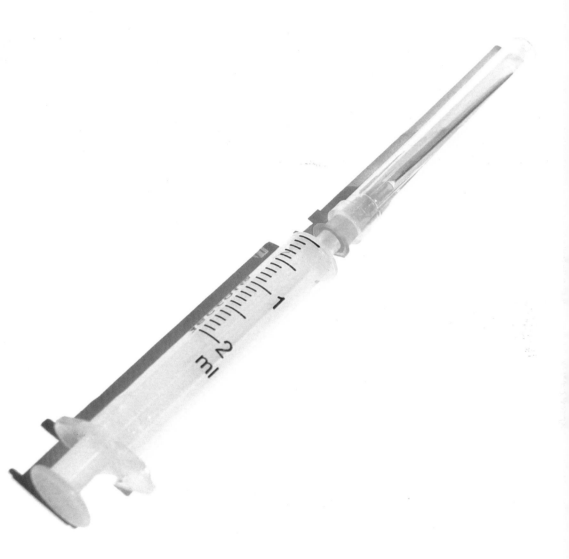

If a meth user injects with a used needle, he puts himself at risk of getting HIV, the virus that causes AIDS.

Someone who uses meth may abuse another drug as well. For many, alcohol is their drug of choice.

bodies. Lead is one of the most common toxins found in meth supplies and can cause death if ingested in large amounts.

The behavioral effects of meth concern other people besides the user. Since the drug produces aggression and violent thoughts, a person on meth is at a higher risk of being involved in criminal behavior such as an assault or murder. He or she has less control over thoughts and actions, and as a result, is less inhibited and may make rash and dangerous decisions. People are also willing to steal or injure to get the object of their addiction. Violence and theft related to any drug, including meth, is fairly ordinary. Accidents, especially those involving automobiles, are also a cause of concern. Like those who drink alcohol and then drive, people who are high on meth while driving also pose a danger to drivers who share the road with them. They don't have the proper mental stability to make accurate decisions or respond quickly while driving.

Heightened Danger

The users of meth are often also users of other drugs. Often, the same people who abuse meth also use alcohol, heroin, cocaine, and marijuana. When these drugs are used in conjunction, the effects of both are multiplied. Many of the deaths involving meth also involve the use of another drug. Combining meth with legal drugs is just as dangerous as taking meth along with other illegal drugs. **Monoamine oxidase inhibitors (MAOIs)**, drugs used to treat depression, are particularly harmful if used conjointly with meth.

Meth use can also lead to other types of addiction. In order to combat the nervousness and tenseness induced

Meth withdrawal can cause extreme emotional and physical reactions. Some individuals may even have thoughts of suicide.

by methamphetamine, some people may begin taking anxiety-reducing drugs such as benzodiazepines rather than stop taking the drug originally causing the problem. Instead of battling one life-threatening addiction, they are then faced with two.

Women who use meth while pregnant or breast-feeding put their children at risk, as well as themselves. Meth use during pregnancy endangers the unborn baby and can result in spontaneous abortion, premature birth, and low birth weight. Meth may also impact children beyond birth. The drug can be transferred from mother to baby if the baby breastfeeds while the mother is taking meth, and there is also evidence that permanent *neurological* damage may occur if a mother takes meth while pregnant.

Withdrawal

Being addicted to meth is dangerous; in many ways, deciding to stop taking it is equally so. Withdrawal symptoms, or those experienced by a person after stopping the use of a drug, can be serious. A person going through meth withdrawal may feel severely depressed, irritable, and *lethargic*. Again, as when a person is recovering from a meth high, sometimes these feelings can be extreme and can result in violent or suicidal thoughts. Physically, he may experience a loss of energy, insomnia, shaking, nausea, sweating, and hyperventilation. Usually these effects last for a short time, but a period of years may be required for certain users to successfully rid themselves of their addiction. Even after withdrawal, the signs of meth use may permanently remain, such as some forms of brain damage.

4 What Are the Legal Consequences of Using Methamphetamine?

Eric Stone told Partnership for a Drug-Free America about his experiences with meth:

I grew up in the small town of Brandon, South Dakota, a suburb of Sioux Falls. My town is a nice, close-knit community that seemed like a perfect place to raise children—it has even been rated one of the "nicest places to live in America." When I was nine, my father died of a stroke. My mom remarried a year and a half later, and I never got along with my step-father, whom she later divorced. Besides this, I tried to have a normal childhood. I played soccer, football, and wrestled, and I continued to play competitively until I started to use drugs. By my freshman year in high school, I dropped out of all of them.

The First Time

When I first started high school I found what I thought to be the greatest release of my life: marijuana. The first time I got high I felt as if I had finally found what I was looking for—I don't even know what it was. I think I was satisfying some innate teenage curiosity.

I also began to use and abuse LSD, cocaine, alcohol, acid, cough syrup—and methamphetamine. I liked the way drugs made me think, feel and behave. They gave me a false sense of security. No matter what was going wrong in my life, when I got high, it all went away. Drugs also helped me make friends and gain popularity in school. Although I had part-time jobs, besides a CD player for my truck, all my money went to drugs and drug paraphernalia.

My Meth Battle

I remember hearing about "crank" on the news but it wasn't a reality for me until I went over to a friend's house one night and saw him smoking something out of a light bulb. I was shocked because I had always thought that hard drugs were only in big cities. Once I saw my friend doing meth I wanted to try it too.

When I first smoked it, I didn't notice the effects too much—it's not like being drunk where you feel inhibited. I felt amped up. As I continued to use, meth gave me energy and alertness—I could stay up for days and days and not feel fatigued in any way. I also used it as a way out of

Not everyone who uses drugs got their start with illegal substances. Some began with items found in many home medicine cabinets, such as cough syrup.

Methamphetamine—Unsafe Speed   69

Using meth doesn't always mean getting a pleasant high. Instead, fear and even paranoia can result.

dealing with stressful situations. For example, if I had upset a friend for some reason, I could blame it on meth and therefore not have to take responsibility for my actions. At the time I didn't think I was addicted, but now I know that I was from that first moment I tried it.

A Devastating Event

I had a group of friends and we did everything together. Two of them, Eric and Angie, were dating and decided to go out to celebrate their one-year anniversary. That was the only night when we weren't hanging out together, and it was the one night that something terrible happened. On their way home from a restaurant they were hit by a drunk driver and killed.

I was completely devastated. Nothing mattered to me anymore—especially my grades. After their death my new best friend became meth. And we started hanging out every night.

Becoming Addicted

It wasn't long after I started using meth that I could no longer get high like I used to. Instead, I got paranoid, scared, and uncomfortable and I started distancing myself from friends and family. I was caught for stealing, possession of marijuana and numerous underage-consumption violations. I found myself in and out of juvenile detention centers and rehab clinics and I still thought the answer was in drugs. I just kept thinking I was different in some way because all my friends seemed to be able to handle the drugs just fine. (Turns out I was wrong—to this day, many of them are addicted.)

I thought that maybe I wasn't using the right stuff, maybe I wasn't using enough, maybe I wasn't using it the right way, maybe I needed to be more careful so I wouldn't get caught. Quitting seemed impossible because I couldn't imagine my life without drugs. By eighteen, I was spiritually dead. I had experienced many bad highs and bad trips, dropped out of high school, lost my popularity and friends and spent most of my time isolating myself in my room using more drugs.

My Mom's Reaction

After losing her trust, stealing from her and lying to her face, my mom tried to kick me out numerous times, but I would never listen to her until she filed a restraining order against me. I was forced out of my home by the police and told that I was not welcome back anytime soon. I had dropped out of school by my sophomore year, and I was homeless. I was unable to find a shelter and spent a couple nights sleeping behind a local church until I finally found a shed. I was hungry, tired and lonely.

On one particular occasion I tried to sneak in my house when my mom caught me and called the police. I quickly hid behind some bushes in the neighbor's yard waiting for the police to leave so I could try to sneak in again. As I watched the house I noticed one of the officers carrying out

Using drugs can make one say or do something the person wouldn't under ordinary circumstances. This can cause her to become alienated from friends and family.

Methamphetamine—Unsafe Speed 73

Drug use and arrest often go hand in hand. For many, this is their first time on the wrong side of the legal system.

some stereo equipment that I had recently stolen. I knew right away I was in big trouble. I soon had a new home: the county jail.

Jail Time

The cops uncovered everything I had stolen and quickly found the shed where I was living and arrested me on a number of charges, for which I faced a total of sixty-five years in prison.

Once in jail, I entered a treatment program, even though I had no desire to stop using. A month later, an inmate called me into his cell and told me he had a little "care package" that he wanted me to bring in. A couple weeks later I had successfully snuck meth and seven hits of LSD into the county jail. (Wondering how I did this? When I left the jail each day to attend treatment, someone would meet me with the drugs. I hid them in a hole I'd made in my boxer shorts. I couldn't imagine doing something like that today but then it seemed like a really good idea.)

One night I was breaking up a line of meth on the mirrored metal of my desk in my cell. It was dark and I couldn't really tell how big the line was. It proved to be too much. I overdosed and went into a psychosis for the next four days. I hallucinated and heard voices. I thought cellmates were talking to me when they really weren't—I tried to have "conversations" with the voices I heard. For days I was out of touch with reality and trapped inside my own, drug-induced, scary world. After that experience even my cellmates were telling me that I should quit.

A prison or jail sentence can follow a drug arrest. For some, this can be the start to turning around their lives.

My Moment of Truth

One of my turning points occurred four months into my jail term at my sentencing hearing. I had been kicked out of treatment though and had spent 30 days in the "hole," so it seemed likely that I would sit the full year. I had gotten my GED while I was in jail, however, so that looked good for my case. For whatever reason the judge gave me a second chance and I was sentenced to six months in jail and required to successfully complete another treatment program after release.

After getting out of jail I was able to stay clean by isolating myself. I wouldn't talk to anyone. I would go to work (I was a night janitor at a grocery store), come home, go to bed, then wake up and repeat the same cycle again. I did this for a while and things seemed to be getting a little better. I

Having a job can help recovering addicts stay off drugs. It occupies their time and helps develop good self-esteem.

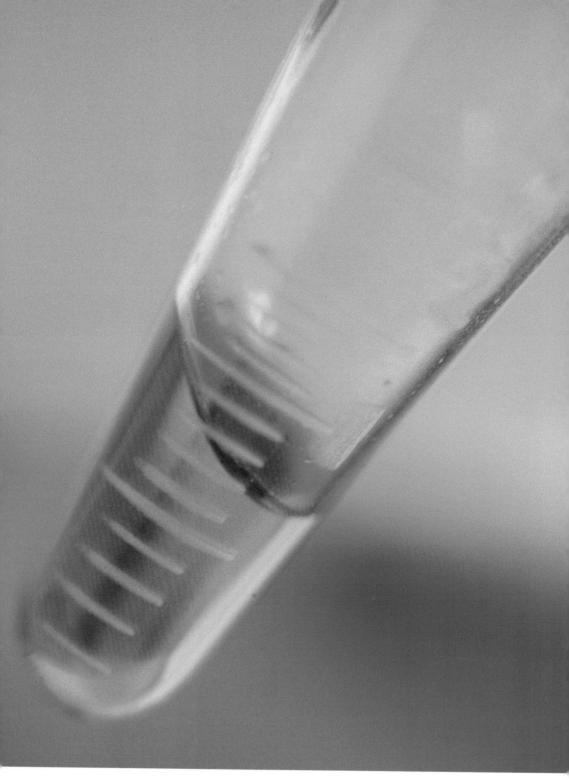

As a condition of parole or probation, individuals may be required to submit their urine for random drug testing.

was clean and I had some money saved up in the bank.

Then I met a guy at work who had the "hook-up." He invited me over after work and I remember telling myself I wasn't going to use—I was just going to hang out. Once we got over to his place and they started passing meth around I was unable to say no. I had to have it. I knew I had to see my probation officer in four days and I remember thinking that meth only stays in your system for three days. I decided to use. Three days later I found myself in the same basement. I couldn't stop using, even though I knew I had to see my P.O. I ended up sitting in that basement for three days straight and never left—high the entire time.

I still made it into my PO's office—dirty and praying he wouldn't ask for a urine analysis. We talked for a bit and just before I thought he was going to set up our next appointment he asked, "Well, Eric, how about a UA?" My eyes grew big. I could tell by his stare that he knew what I knew. Then he said, "Get outta here, we'll get you next time." I later found out that he was leaving his job and didn't want to send anyone back to prison on his last couple of days. I thank God for that second chance.

Why I Changed

I was sick of hurting all the time and sick and tired of the addiction. I had experienced too much pain in my life, and doing drugs was no longer something that gave me pleasure—it was something

A history of drug addiction does not doom one to a life of failure. Many recovering addicts graduate from college, and some become drug counselors to help others kick the habit.

that controlled my life. After getting a new probation officer who would make me go to twelve-step meetings numerous times a week, I relapsed one last time. Then I put everything I had into focusing on a recovery. So far, it's worked.

My Life Today

Today my existence has been revolutionized. I no longer have the obsession to use drugs and I have been clean and sober for over two-and-a-half years. I graduated from college with a 3.9 GPA and received an associate's degree in Chemical

Dependency Counseling. I was inducted into an international honor society and was flown to Boston to receive a $2,000 scholarship and national recognition as a nominee for the All-USA Academic Team. I have been employed for the last three years and currently work at an adolescent drug treatment center. I have recently been accepted into one of the country's top ten universities where I will be working on my bachelor's degree in Psychology and Addiction Studies. Today I have a deep compassion for those who struggle with addiction. By helping others I help myself, which is one of the stones in my foundation of recovery.

Meth addiction is cunning and baffling. It starts out as a harmless and fun thing to do and then, before you know it, your whole life becomes centered on it and it gets to the point where you can't imagine life without it. But you're unable to live with it.

I have developed some strong and meaningful friendships since getting clean. I have repaired my relationship with my mother, and she has accepted me back into her home and her life. As horrible as

The Drug Scheduling system was put into effect in 1970. It categorizes all controlled drugs or substances on which legal limits must be placed into five schedules because of the risk of addiction and dependency. Schedule I drugs, including heroin and marijuana, are considered high-risk drugs with no accepted medical use. Schedule II substances have a high-risk association, but also have an accepted use for medicinal purposes. Schedule III, IV, and V drugs are all substances that must be controlled, but have a wider variety of legitimate medical purposes. Schedule V contains over-the-counter drugs. The lower schedules include barbiturates, painkillers, and cough medicine.

my experience was, the one good thing that has come from it is the new appreciation I have for life today.

The costs of abusing drugs like meth are not limited to physical and mental deterioration. In many cases, people must also deal with the law and the consequences of their actions in a legal context.

Currently, methamphetamine is classified as a Schedule II drug in the United States. This means that it has a high potential for abuse and dependency, but also has an accepted medical use. Other drugs in this category include morphine and cocaine.

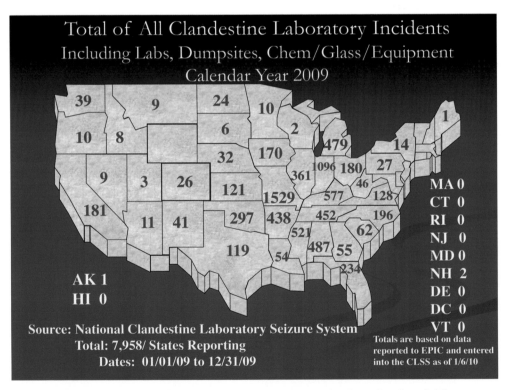

New laws give law enforcement increased power to shut down illegal meth labs. The controversial PATRIOT Act puts restrictions on the purchase of everyday ingredients used to make meth.

Laws at All Levels of the Government

Since the Controlled Substance Act of 1970, which placed limitations on the manufacture of meth and other drugs, additional laws have been put in place in an effort to combat meth abuse. The Comprehensive Methamphetamine Control Act of 1996 gave police the right to domestically seize chemicals involved in the manufacture of meth, making meth lab seizures and cleanups easier. It also imposed harsher and longer penalties for those found in possession of meth or the equipment used to make it. Currently, possession of ten grams of meth results in five years in prison, while possession of one hundred grams equals at least ten years in prison.

In July 2000, the Methamphetamine Anti-Proliferation Act was passed. It built upon the limitations set up by the Control Act of 1996, backing the training of law enforcement in meth lab investigations and cleanup, responding to the growing number of meth lab incidents around the country. In addition, it limited the production and sale of some of the chemicals used in meth production, discouraging manufacturers from buying them.

The PATRIOT Act, in an updated version signed by President George W. Bush in 2006, restricted the sale and purchase of ephedrine and pseudoephedrine. These two chemicals, found in many common cold medicines, are often used in the production of meth. The new laws require that medicines containing these chemicals be moved behind drugstore counters, and limit the amount of each medicine that one person can purchase at a time. Additionally, several millions of dollars were allotted for meth addiction research, education in meth abuse, and law enforcement.

At the local and state levels, laws restricting the sale and availability of *precursor* chemicals, or those substances that are involved in the manufacture of meth, were enacted well before the addition to the PATRIOT Act was put in place. For example, both Oregon and Mississippi, as well as several cities have laws restricting the sale of ephedrine and psuedoephedrine (precursor chemicals). They make it more difficult for manufacturers to buy the necessary ingredients to make their product, although producers can get around these laws by purchasing the chemicals in an area that doesn't have laws that are as stringent.

For example, in Iowa, it is illegal to possess or sell meth, produce meth, and/or to possess ephedrine or pseudoephedrine with the intent to make meth or to give it to someone who will use it to make meth. A person can be sentenced up to a year in jail if found in possession of the drug. A person who sells meth or is in possession of meth with the intent to sell it can be sentenced to ten to fifty years in jail and fined up to one million dollars. If that same person produced meth in front of a minor, five years will be added on to the sentence. Other states, especially those in the Midwest, have similar laws mandating what is illegal and the punishments that can be dealt out to those who violate them.

Run-Ins with the Law

Legal problems dealing with meth are not just about possession or trafficking. Because of the effects that meth has on behavior, a person high on meth may become involved in violent crimes or other criminal activity. For example, meth is increasingly involved with growing numbers of domestic violence incidents and child abandonment. Meth takes over addicts' lives, leaving them unable to care for children or other members of their households.

Additionally, because of an addict's need for meth, he or she may resort to violent behavior or theft to get it. Meth is an expensive habit to maintain. Prices fluctuate over the years, rising when new laws are enacted and precursor chemicals are harder to buy. Prices also vary from region to region. Meth is generally cheaper in western states, because it is more readily available, and more expensive in the eastern United States. In 2009, the average price for pure methamphetamine was $127.28 for one gram, which was 13.5 percent less than in 2007. At the same time, the average purity increased.

In data collected in a 2003 National Drug Threat Assessment, approximately 32 percent of state and local law enforcement agencies throughout the country cited meth as the drug that was involved the most in violent criminal activity. Jails across the country report that a significant percentage of their inmates are imprisoned for reasons directly or indirectly related to meth, whether for posses-

The legal system realizes that jail or prison is not the best alternative for all people facing drug charges. Drug courts encourage rehabilitation, which can be very successful.

sion, running a lab, or assaulting someone while under the influence of meth. In a study done in 2005 by the National Association of Counties, half of the counties surveyed indicated that up to 20 percent of all inmates were in jail because of meth.

Drug Courts: An Alternative to Jail

Although possession or use of meth usually results in jail time, there are other options for some found guilty of that crime. Drug courts have been developed in recent years for nonviolent drug addicts as substitutes for prison. Instead of sitting in jail, participants in the drug court system are sent to rehabilitation programs. They must agree to stop taking drugs, face random drug testing, and work cooperatively with their rehabilitators. In return, drug courts provide intensive support and counseling to help convicts achieve drug-free lives. If a person is able to complete the program successfully, the charges against him or her may be dropped, depending on the seriousness of the offense committed.

In general, drug courts have a high success rate. Participants are closely monitored and given crucial support. Skipping jail time is a good incentive for some to stop taking drugs. In the case of meth, which is particularly difficult to quit using, the fact that participants are forced to cease use is one of the reasons for drug courts' success. It has been found that the likelihood that those who complete the program become involved in criminal activity is reduced, as is later drug use after completion.

5 Controversial Issues

According to journalist Sarah Fenske of the *Phoenix New Times*, Arizona's government was convinced that if they cut the supply of the ingredients used to make crystal meth—namely, cold medicines—the demand would drop as well.

But when a law went into effect that regulated all cold medicines containing pseudoephedrine—one of the key ingredients meth cooks use—the results took by them surprise. Under the new law, everything from Sudafed to Tylenol Cold has to be kept behind the counter, and customers must sign a logbook that is faxed monthly to the police.

As the cops read through the logs, they kept noticing the same name over and over at the same address in a small town outside Phoenix. So the police went out to investigate. They were ready to bust a ring of meth cookers.

Instead, they found a large family with the flu.

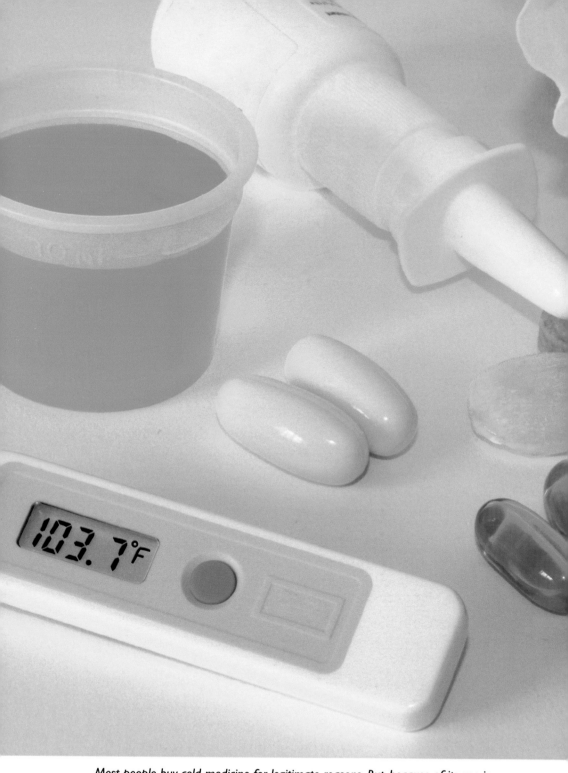

Most people buy cold medicine for legitimate reasons. But, because of its use in making illegal meth, laws have been passed controlling who can purchase it and how much can be bought.

According to the *New Times*, police didn't find the logbooks to be much help in leading them to meth cooks, nor did the new law do much to cut the demand for meth. Turned out, most Arizona addicts were now purchasing their meth from Mexican dealers, who made a cheaper, more potent recipe than the homegrown domestic labs did.

As a result, when folks in Arizona talked about how to handle the meth problem, they were no longer discussing cold medicines; instead, they started talking about treatment and prevention.

Meanwhile, though, the federal government was still focused on cold medicines. The PATRIOT Act included a set of provisions that regulated pseudoephedrine, setting the purchase limit at nine grams per customer per month. It also required that medications with that ingredient be kept behind the counter, and customers had to sign a logbook.

Not everyone was convinced that the government was looking at the meth problem from the right perspective. Like the people in Arizona, many Americans were wondering whether prevention and treatment was more effective than laws that regulate meth production.

Meth is a big problem. Something has to be done about it. But people don't agree yet on exactly what that thing should be. The situation is far more complicated than cold medicines.

As with any drug, methamphetamine directly harms the person who uses it. However, meth also causes more than its share of indirect harm on others, making it one of the most dangerous drugs being used today. Besides putting those in contact with meth abusers at risk, home laboratories also place many other people in danger, including those who have no direct contact with users.

For example, in February 2012, a meth lab exploded in an apartment building in the Tulsa, Oklahoma, area. Although luckily no one was hurt in the explosion, the entire building was contaminated, forcing people out of their homes. All too often, an explosion of this sort does injure or kill people living near the site of the blast. This situation isn't rare either; meth labs are quickly becoming a significant danger to society, everywhere from big cities to small towns.

Meth Labs: Health Risks

The labs where meth is synthesized are dangerous mainly because of the flammable toxic materials that are involved. According to the National Clandestine Laboratory Seizure System, there were 529 reported meth lab fires or explosions in 2003, and it has only gotten worse since then. In fact, according to the United States Department of Justice, about fifteen percent of meth labs are discovered because of fire or explosion. These accidents happen because many of the chemicals used in meth production are *combustible* and are handled or stored in an unsafe manner.

The chemicals involved in meth production are also dangerous on their own, not just because of the risk of fire. The substances used to make meth and those produced as unwanted by-products are as harmful, or more so, than the desired meth itself. Prolonged exposure can cause respiratory problems like shortness of breath, chest pain, and coughing. Dizziness, headaches, and nausea can also occur. The severity of these symptoms varies based on the amount of toxins a person is exposed to, as well as the length of time spent in contact with them. If the exposure is serious enough, liver damage and cancer become major health risks.

Of course, the people who are in the most danger are the producers themselves due to the amount of time they spend working with the chemicals. However, other people who live near the meth lab, which is often set up in a

Not all meth labs are stationary. They have been discovered in trailers and even in the trunks of cars.

Meth labs are filled with toxic chemicals that can stay on surfaces for months, even years. They have given birth to a specialized, meth lab cleanup industry.

residential home, are also placed in harm's way, most unknowingly. Labs are especially unsafe for young children, since they do not understand the danger involved with handling the chemicals that may be stored out in the open. Children also have the most vulnerable immune systems, placing them at even greater risk for chemical poisoning. The toxins from meth production can remain on surfaces like clothing and furniture for months, exposing people to danger for an extended period.

Other people have to be concerned with the health effects of meth labs as well. Anyone who comes in contact with manufacturers, including law officials, jail personnel, hospital workers, and rehabilitation staff, is in danger. Even people who live in former lab sites can experience health problems long after the lab itself has been shut down. Because proper meth lab cleanup is not always completed, the home or business can remain contaminated by chemicals without the knowledge of the home or business owners.

Meth Lab Cleanup

Cleanup is a dangerous process that nonetheless needs to be done to prevent any further contamination of the property and to prevent future explosions. After the lab is discovered and shut down, the first step is to call in a hazardous materials crew. The crew removes the lab equipment after having begun to air out the lab site. They also remove chemicals still in containers and any items that appear to have been contaminated. Sometimes the building must be sealed and heated for several days to get rid of remaining chemicals. Airing out the site continues for three to five more days, but it is a process that could take weeks and yet never be completely successful.

Common Odors Associated with a Methamphetamine Lab

ether
solvents
vinegar
ammonia
airplane glue
boat resin
acetone
sweet plastic
pungent odors like dirty diapers
cat litter or cat urine

Cleaning materials that could absorb chemical vapors is also very important. Carpets, furniture, clothes, and walls can all retain chemicals if they are not cleaned or disposed of properly. Ventilation systems in the site need to be replaced as well, since chemicals can become trapped there and reenter the building. Even plumbing systems must sometimes be replaced if the manufacturer used sinks or toilets to dispose of the by-products of production.

Once the site is safe to occupy again, regular household cleaning should be done using water and detergent. It is also usually a good idea to put fresh coats of paint on walls and ceilings to lock in any chemicals that could still be lingering on surfaces.

Meth Labs Don't Just Pose Danger to People

Environmental damage is another concern associated with meth labs. The production of meth involves many chemicals of varying *toxicity*, from acetone to hydrochloric acid. It also creates several by-products, besides meth, that are undesired and that must be disposed of safely. As many as six pounds of waste are produced for every pound of meth that is synthesized. Meth producers are generally unable to dispose of these leftovers properly and often pour them down drains or into the ground. The waste may no longer directly be the producers' problem, but it contaminates drinking water, soil, and waterways. Additionally, besides the obvious harm done to the environment and people's health, toxic meth waste is expensive and can cost millions of dollars per year to clean up, which becomes the burden of taxpayers. The proper cleanup of just one lab can cost up to $150,000.

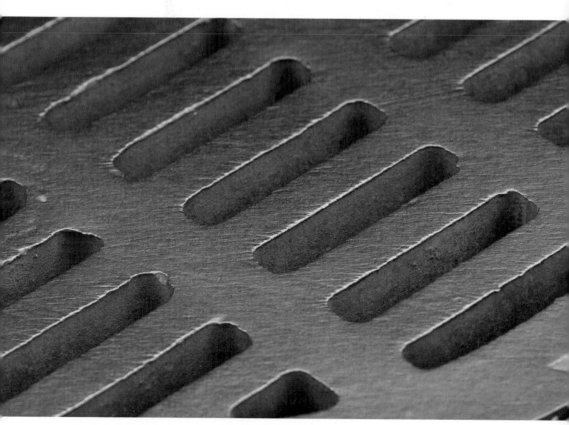

Pouring chemicals down the drain and into the sewage system will produce long-lasting ill effects far from the site of the meth lab.

The Role of Drug Companies

In order to control meth abuse, laws have been enacted restricting the sale of precursor chemicals, especially ephedrine and pseudoephedrine. While the drug companies that produce over-the-counter medicines containing these chemicals have made some efforts to aid in the fight against meth abuse, some people want them to do more.

Pfizer, the company that makes Sudafed®, came out with a new medicine, Sudafed PE. This newer version does not contain pseudoephedrine like the original, causing many people to applaud their efforts in fighting against meth production. However, Pfizer is still selling Sudafed, allowing meth producers easy access to the necessary precursor chemical. Those opposed to companies like Pfizer want to see them work harder to combat meth abuse, rather than focus on profits. They believe that government regulations are not enough to curb what is seen as a national epidemic; drug companies must join the fight as well.

Legalizing Meth

Like those involved with the more famous movement to legalize marijuana, there is a small number of people who want to reduce or eliminate restrictions on the use of methamphetamine. While not denying the harm that the drug can have, some cite the importance of the freedom to choose what to do with one's own body and claim that allowing the government to regulate that freedom is unconstitutional.

This group directly contrasts with those who believe that the only way of dealing with meth abuse is to create stricter laws dealing with the issue. Because meth is made

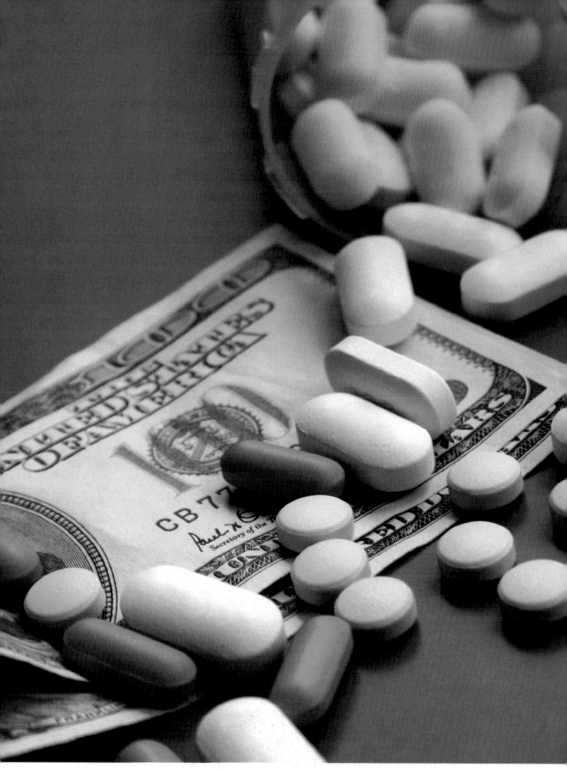

Despite all that is known about the cooking of illegal meth, some pharmaceutical companies continue to produce medications used by these infamous chefs. After all, cold and allergy medications bring a lot of money to drug companies.

Methamphetamine—Unsafe Speed   99

Because everyday ingredients are used in making illegal meth, limiting access to these products—locking them up—may be the best option in curtailing illegal meth production.

from preexisting chemicals, the easiest way to prevent abuse is to place tighter restrictions on those chemicals, making it harder for people to make the drug. Unlike other drugs such as cocaine, which are derived naturally and whose production is harder to control, meth abuse can be stopped at its source.

This country may not have come to a definitive conclusion on how to deal with the growing methamphetamine crisis, but most people will agree that there is a problem. The detrimental effects that meth abuse has on individuals and society as a whole will continue to increase unless people are made aware of the drug's dangers and work together to end it.

6 Treatment

Remember Maggie from chapter 1? She ended up staying with a group of people in New York City, where she smoked meth every day, week after week. Finally, though, her parents tracked her down. They brought her home, and then the entire family sat down in the living room together. They agreed they needed help.

Maggie's parents and her little brother went for counseling. Her father started going to Alcoholics Anonymous. And Maggie enrolled in a drug rehabilitation program. She lived at home and attended sessions every day. She signed a pact with her family that she would stop using speed.

But that wasn't the end of her problems. Quitting meth wasn't easy. She relapsed once—and then again. Finally, though, forty-five days went by, forty-five days that Maggie was meth-free. Maggie knew she wasn't home free yet, but she had come far enough now that she didn't want to lose the ground she had gained.

Having close friends is important throughout life. They can help keep one on a drug-free path.

With her counselor's help, she made a list of warning signs that her parents should watch for, signs that would tell them she was heading toward a relapse. These signs included:

- not going to her rehab sessions
- acting angry or depressed
- hanging out with her old friends
- staying out late

Almost every family faces conflict at some time. If family members are willing to work on their relationships, they may be able to weather the storm.

Meanwhile, the rehab program referred Maggie to a psychiatrist, who diagnosed Maggie with both depression and attention-deficit with hyperactivity disorder. The psychiatrist began treating Maggie for both conditions, which helped her be less vulnerable to her cravings for meth.

Finally, Maggie made it through an entire year without using meth. She finished high school, and she was

The Twelve Steps

1. We admitted we were powerless over our addiction, that our lives had become unmanageable.
2. Came to believe that a Power greater than ourselves could restore us to sanity.
3. Made a decision to turn our will and our lives over to the care of God as we understood God.
4. Made a searching and fearless moral inventory of ourselves.
5. Admitted to God, to ourselves and to another human being the exact nature of our wrongs.
6. Were entirely ready to have God remove all these defects of character.
7. Humbly asked God to remove our shortcomings.
8. Made a list of all persons we had harmed, and became willing to make amends to them all.
9. Made direct amends to such people wherever possible, except when to do so would injure them or others.
10. Continued to take personal inventory and when we were wrong promptly admitted it.
11. Sought through prayer and meditation to improve our conscious contact with God as we understood God, praying only for knowledge of God's will for us and the power to carry that out.
12. Having had a spiritual awakening as the result of these steps, we tried to carry this message to other addicts, and to practice these principles in all our affairs.

Musician Fergie struggled with a meth addiction, but through rehabilitation was able to overcome her addiction.

Kicking meth is hard, and recovering users often fall into a deep depression. In some cases, individuals can't handle the depression and return to using drugs.

heading for college. Her parents were working with her to change the way they lived, and to make those changes permanent. The treatment process was hard work for them all.

Meth addiction is one of the hardest drug habits to break. There are no known chemical treatments available to those who want to end their addiction, so complete **ces-sation** is the only path to take. The depression experienced by those in withdrawal is so severe as to cause many people to resume taking meth, resulting in a very low success rate in treatment. However, there are services that can help an addict recover for good. Cognitive behavioral therapy, which is meant to change the way a person thinks and behaves, has been found to be successful. Group therapy is also successful, especially when it involves an entire family who works together to help one or more members overcome their addiction.

The largest program to help meth users quit is called Crystal Meth Anonymous. Like Alcoholics Anonymous, the group uses a series of twelve steps that help users overcome their addictions. Other kinds of therapy also work toward the same goal.

Relapse Prevention Therapy

In relapse therapy, patients learn to build self-control skills by recognizing and correcting problem behaviors. Specific techniques include weighing the positive and negative consequences of continued drug use, self-monitoring in order to identify high-risk situations for use, and developing methods used for coping with or avoiding those situations.

Achieving a series of smaller goals can help one reach the big, long-term goal of living drug free.

In Motivational Enhancement Therapy, individuals are encouraged to develop skills necessary to staying away from drugs.

Motivational Enhancement Therapy

For individuals who feel **ambivalent** about treatment, this approach aims to quickly motivate patients into discontinuing drug use. The therapy consists of an initial assessment battery session followed by two to four individual treatment sessions with a therapist. The first session attempts to get the patient to come up with self-motivational statements and a plan for change that includes suggested strategies for coping with high-risk situations. In subsequent meetings, the therapist monitors change, reviews cessation strategies being used, and continues to encourage commitment to change or sustain abstinence. Patients are sometimes also encouraged to bring a significant other to sessions.

What Do Rehab Programs Accomplish?

Abstinence

In many cases it seems that as long as the substance is in the blood stream, thinking remains distorted. Often during the first days or weeks of total abstinence, we see a gradual clearing of thinking processes. This is a complex psychological and biological phenomenon, and is one of the elements that inpatient programs are able to provide by making sure the patient is fully detoxified and remains abstinent during his or her stay.

Removal of Denial

In some cases, when someone other than the patient, such as a parent, employer, or other authority, is convinced there is a problem, but the addict is not yet sure, voluntary attendance at a rehab program will provide enough clarification to remove this basic denial. Even those who are convinced they have a problem with substances usually don't admit to themselves or others the full extent of the addiction. Rehab uses group process to identify and help the individual to let go of these expectable forms of denial.

Removal of Isolation

As addictions progress, relationships deteriorate in quality. However, the bonds between fellow recovering people are widely recognized as one of the few forces powerful enough to keep recovery on track. The rehab experience, whether it is inpatient or outpatient involves in-depth sharing in a group setting. This kind of sharing creates strong interpersonal bonds among group members. These bonds help to form a support system that will be powerful enough to sustain the individual during the first months of abstinence.

"Basic Training"

Basic training is a good way to think of the experience of rehab. Soldiers need a rapid course to give them the basic knowledge and skills they will need to fight in a war. Some kinds of learning need to be practiced so well that you can do them without thinking. In addition to the learning, trainees become physically fit, and perhaps most important, form emotional bonds that help keep up morale when the going is hard.

(Source: Partnership for a Drug-Free America)

Attending a support group can increase the possibility of a successful recovery and of repairing damaged relationships.

Individual and group counseling sessions can help in recovery success. Underlying reasons for addiction can be explored and new ways of coping developed.

Rehabilitation or "rehab" programs traditionally have the following basic elements:
- initial evaluation
- abstinence
- learning about addiction
- group counseling
- AA or other Twelve-Step participation
- individual counseling
- a family program

Supportive Expressive Therapy

Designed to help patients feel comfortable in relating their personal experiences and to identify and work through their interpersonal relationship issues, this therapy approach allows participants to explore ways to solve problem feelings and behaviors without falling back on previous addictive behaviors.

Individualized Drug Counseling

This approach helps patients develop coping skills and other strategies in order to stop drug use and achieve total abstinence. Twelve-step participation is encouraged, along with other services that address other problem issues such as employment status, illegal activity, and family and social relationships. Counseling sessions are usually scheduled one to two times a week.

Matrix Model

The matrix model incorporates several treatment methods, including relapse prevention, family and group therapies, drug education, and self-help participation. It also

Recovery begins for some with a hospital stay. Eventually, treatment moves to an outpatient basis.

offers education for family members affected by the addiction. However, this treatment method relies most heavily on relationships forged between patient and therapist. Acting as a teacher and coach, therapists educate patients about issues critical to addiction and relapse, and attempt to raise the patient's self-esteem, dignity, and self-worth through continual encouragement and positive reinforcement of desired behavioral changes. Maintaining a positive relationship is vitally important for keeping the patient involved in the program.

Behavioral Therapy for Adolescents

Behavioral therapy tries to help young patients by teaching them to

- exert control by avoiding situations associated with drug use.
- recognize and change negative thoughts, feelings, or plans that lead to drug use.
- enlist family and friends to help them stay away from drugs.

Therapeutic activities may include fulfilling specific assignments, rehearsing desired behaviors. and recording and reviewing progress. Praises and privileges are consistently given as positive reinforcements for meeting assigned goals and demonstrating desired behaviors.

Multidimensional Family Therapy (MDFT) for Adolescents

Outpatient drug abuse treatment positively utilizes the network of influences on youth behavior by incorporating family as an active part of therapy. During individual and family sessions, therapists help develop the skills that enable teenagers to cope with life's stresses. Therapists also teach parents ways to improve their parenting. Young patients attempt to better their decision-making, negotiation, problem-solving, and communication skills, while parents work to positively influence their children.

Recovery from meth addiction is not easy. There is no miraculous treatment program that will quickly and simply take away an addict's craving for meth. But recovery is possible. As with any addiction, the first step is to recognize the problem—and then seek help.

Glossary

ambivalent: Having mixed, uncertain, or conflicting feelings about something.

athetosis: A condition characterized by involuntary slow movements of the extremities and usually caused by a brain lesion.

blue-collar: Relating to workers who do manual or industrial work.

cessation: A temporary or final end to an action.

chronic: Long-term or frequently recurring.

combustible: Able or likely to catch fire.

dilated: Became wider or larger.

epidemiology: The scientific and medical study of the causes and transmission of diseases within a population.

euphoria: A feeling of extreme happiness.

lethargic: Slow, sluggish, lazy.

metabolism: The series of chemical reactions taking place in living organisms that break down nutrients to provide the energy necessary to sustain life.

monoamine oxidase inhibitors (MAOIs): Antidepressant drugs that work by blocking the breakdown of monoamines in the brain.

narcolepsy: A condition characterized by frequent, brief, uncontrollable episodes of deep sleep, sometimes with hallucinations and an inability to move.

neurological: Relating to the nervous system.

neurons: Cells that transmit nerve impulses.

precursor: Something that comes before and leads to the development of another thing.

psychosis: A psychiatric disorder that is marked by delusions, hallucinations, and a distorted sense of reality.

rave parties: Large-scale parties or club events at which music is played that last sometimes all night.

schizophrenia: A psychiatric condition characterized by a loss of contact with reality.

synthesized: Created by combining diverse elements.

toxicity: The degree to which something is poisonous.

vascular: Relating to the circulatory system which transports blood around the body.

Further Reading

Erdmann, Larry R. *Methamphetamine: The Drug of Death*. Lincoln, Neb.: iUniverse, 2006.

Johnson, Dirk. *Meth: America's Home-Cooked Menace*. Hazelden, Minn.: Hazelden Publishing and Educational Services, 2005.

Lee, Steven. *Overcoming Crystal Meth Addiction*. Emeryville, Calif.: Avalon, 2006.

Littell, Mary Ann. *Speed and Methamphetamine Drug Dangers*. Berkeley Heights, N.J.: Enslow, 2005.

Marcovitz, Hal. *Methamphetamine*. Farmington Hills, Mich.: Thomson Gale, 2005.

Mintzer, Rich. *Meth and Speed = Busted*. Berkeley Heights, N.J.: Enslow, 2005.

For More Information

Go Ask Alice!
www.goaskalice.columbia.edu

NIDA InfoFacts: Methamphetamine
www.nida.nih.gov/infofacts/methamphetamine.html

Partnership for a Drug-Free America
www.drugfree.org

What You Need to Know About Drugs: Methamphetamines
kidshealth.org/kid/grow/drugs_alcohol/know_drugs_meths.html

Bibliography

Braswell, Sterling R. *American Meth: A History of the Methamphetamine Epidemic in America.* Lincoln, Neb.: iUniverse, 2006.

Lower Mainland Assessment and Referral Service
http://www.lmars.com/Crystal-Meth-Across-Canada.htm

Mark, Michelle. "'Long Way to Go' for Meth Treatment Facilities." *Sun News* (Edmonton, Alberta), June 9, 2006.

National Institute on Drug Abuse
http://www.nida.nih.gov/Infofacts/methamphetamine.html

Parker, James N., M.D., and Philip M. Parker, Ph.D. (Eds.). *The Official Patient's Sourcebook on Methamphetamine Dependence.* San Diego, Calif.: ICON Health Publications. 2002.

Parker, James N., and Philip M. Parker. *Methamphetamines: Medical Dictionary, Bibliography, and Annotated Research Guide to Internet References.* San Diego, Calif.: ICON Health Publications, 2004.

Urban 75: Drug Info
http://www.urban75.com/Drugs/meth.html

The websites listed on this page were active at the time of publication. The publisher is not responsible for websites that have changed their addresses or discontinued operation since the date of publication. The publisher will review and update the website list upon each reprint.

Index

abstinence 112
acid 68
addiction 19, 20, 47, 54, 57, 63, 65, 109, 117, 118
aggression 63
alcohol 21, 63, 68
Alcoholics Anonymous 109
Allies 15
amphetamine 15, 16
anti-anxiety medication 60, 63
appetite suppressant 41
Arizona 89, 91
Asia 16
asthma 15
attention deficit disorder 45

behavioral therapy 117
benzodiazepines 63
binge 21, 42, 43
blood pressure 57
brain 57
British Columbia 25
Bush, George W. 16, 83

California 41
Canada 25, 26, 83
categories of users 42
central nervous system 55, 56
chalk 12
cocaine 19, 68, 101
cognitive behavioral therapy 109

Comprehensive Methamphetamine Control Act of 1996 83
Controlled Substance Act of 1970 16, 83
convulsions 55, 60
cough syrup 68, 69
counseling 115
crime 85
Crystal Meth Anonymous 109

dehydration 59
depression 57, 65
Desoxyn 45
dopamine 18, 57
drug companies 98
drug courts 87
Drug Enforcement Agency 84
Drug Scheduling 81

endorphin 19
ephedrine 84, 98
epinephrine 21
euphoria 12, 43

formication 57

Germany 15
glass 12
Great Depression 15

hallucinations 47, 57
Hawaii 42

Picture Credits

Bananastock 110
Brand X Pictures Colin Anderson 56
Comstock 8
Corbis 36, 66, 74, 76, 86
DEA, www.usdoj.gov/dea 14, 23, 82
Image Source 113
istock.com 52, 102
Iwan, Beijes 61
Jupiter Images 10, 13, 22, 31, 32, 40, 52, 58, 62, 77, 78, 80, 88, 90, 93, 94, 97, 99, 100, 111, 114, 116
NIH 18
NOAA 23, 43
Photodisc 44, 69
Photolink 20
Stockbyte 27, 35
stock.xchang 28, 46, 55, 64, 70, 104, 105, 107, 108
Thinkstock 39, 73
US Department of Veterans Affairs 17

To the best knowledge of the publisher, all other images are in the public domain. If any image has been inadvertently uncredited, please notify Harding House Publishing Services, Vestal, New York 13850, so that rectification can be made for future printings.

Author and Consultant Biographies

Author

Kim Etingoff currently lives in Boston, Massachusetts. She grew up in New York State and graduated from the University of Rochester. She has since been pursuing her interests in sustainable farming, nutrition, and writing.

Series Consultant

Jack E. Henningfield, Ph.D., is a professor at the Johns Hopkins University School of Medicine, and he is also Vice President for Research and Health Policy at Pinney Associates, a consulting firm in Bethesda, Maryland, that specializes in science policy and regulatory issues concerning public health, medications development, and behavior-focused disease management. Dr. Henningfield has contributed information relating to addiction to numerous reports of the U.S. Surgeon General, the National Academy of Sciences, and the World Health Organization.